WORLD'S SCARIEST PLACES

CREEPY CEMETERIES

ALIX WOOD

 Gareth Stevens
PUBLISHING

Please visit our website, **www.garethstevens.com**. For a free color catalog of all
our high-quality books, call toll free 1-800-542-2595 or fax 1-877-542-2596.

Cataloging-in-Publication Data
Names: Wood, Alix.
Title: Creepy cemeteries / Alix Wood.
Description: New York : Gareth Stevens, 2017. | Series: World's scariest places | Includes index.
Identifiers: ISBN 9781482459012 (pbk.) | ISBN 9781482459036 (library bound) |
   ISBN 9781482459029 (6 pack)
Subjects: LCSH: Haunted cemeteries--Juvenile literature.
Classification: LCC BF1474.3 W66 2017 | DDC 133.1'22--dc23

First Edition

Published in 2017 by
Gareth Stevens Publishing
111 East 14th Street, Suite 349
New York, NY 10003

Copyright © 2017 Gareth Stevens Publishing

Produced for Gareth Stevens by Alix Wood Books
Designed by Alix Wood
Editor: Eloise Macgregor

Photo credits: Cover, 1 © Dollar Photo Club; 3, 21 © Iain Hinchcliffe; 4, 16 © Shutterstock; 5 top
© William Murphy; 5 bottom © Dan Dee Shots; 6 © Cobra97; 7 © Christine Zenino; 8 © Andrew
Currie; 9 © Tim Adams; 10 © Howard Potts; 10-11 © Nikater; 11 © Harry Burton; 12 © Dauvit
Alexander; 13 © Jonathan Oldenbuck; 14-15 © Garrett Ziegler; 15 top and bottom © public domain;
17 © Sibeaster; 18 © Shutterstock; 19 © Theresa Henry; 20 © Dapog; 22 © rewbs.soal; 23 top and
bottom © Raoul Rodriguez; 24 , 25, 29 © Dreamstime; 26-27 © Goodharbor; 27 © Dana Huff; 28 ©
Quahadi Añtó

Printed in China
CPSIA compliance information: Batch #CW17GS. For further information contact
Gareth Stevens, New York, New York at 1-800-542-2595.

Contents

If you believe that ghosts really exist, then a graveyard is a good place to go looking for some. There are some really spooky cemeteries around the world. When you think that cemeteries are full of dead people, it's hardly surprising that they can be really scary places.

Not everyone believes that places can be haunted. Sometimes a place is just so spooky that you scare yourself even though nothing is really there!

Cemeteries aren't always haunted by dead people. Glasnevin Cemetery in Dublin, Ireland, is said to be home to a ghost Newfoundland dog! Sea captain John McNeill Boyd died in a storm on the Irish Sea. After his funeral, his faithful dog refused to leave his graveside. Eventually starving to death, the dog has been seen haunting the graveyard!

Bachelor's Grove, Chicago

Deep in a lonely woodland on the edge of the city of Chicago lies an overgrown graveyard. Bachelor's Grove Cemetery is said to be one of the most haunted places in America. In the 1960s **vandals** destroyed some of the gravestones. Graves were opened and bones were strewn around the cemetery. Perhaps this made the spirits angry? Since that time there have been many reports of ghostly activity.

It's claimed that a strange red **orb** has been seen flying up and down the trail to the cemetery! There have been reports of a ghostly house, and a black dog, that both disappear in front of people's eyes.

THE HAUNTED POND
AND TURNPIKE

On the turnpike by
Bachelor's Grove, people
claimed they have seen a
car in front of them brake,
turn off, and then disappear!
Others have reported
passing a car which then
vanishes from their
rearview mirror.

At the rear of the
cemetery is a small pond.
In the 1970s, two Forest Preserve officers on
night patrol said they saw a horse pulling a plow
steered by an old man. It lurched out of the water
and crossed the road in front of them, and then
vanished. They later found out that in the 1870s
a farmer had been dragged into the pond and
drowned after his horse had been startled!

La Recoleta Cemetery, Buenos Aires

Built to house the city's wealthy after they passed on, La Recoleta Cemetery has 26 Argentine presidents buried there. There are over 6,400 grand **mausoleums** in the graveyard. Ghosts are said to haunt La Recoleta. The Lady in White is said to **lure** young men to take her on a date. Later, they discover she is actually a ghost from the cemetery.

In the early 1900s a man working in the cemetery saved up to buy a plot and build his own grave. Once everything was ready, he took his own life! Night watchmen have since heard his spirit rattle his keys as he passes.

LA RECOLETA CEMETERY

The most famous ghost said to haunt La Recoleta Cemetery is of a young woman named Rufina Cambaceres. She died suddenly on her 19th birthday. A horse-drawn carriage took her to the cemetery one rainy day in 1902. Due to the weather, the gravediggers left her **casket** in the chapel, to be buried later.

The next morning a worker discovered the casket had moved and its lid was slightly open. Worried her grave had been robbed, her family asked to open the casket. When the lid was lifted, nothing had been stolen, but the inside of the lid had been scratched! Rufina must have not really been dead. Her ghost is now said to haunt the cemetery.

A STATUE OF RUFINA LEAVING HER MAUSOLEUM

The Valley of the Kings, Egypt

It has been said that the tombs of the ancient Egyptian **pharaohs** are cursed. Any person who tries to enter a tomb is believed to suffer a strange death. The Valley of the Kings, near Cairo, was the pharaohs' burial site. Because pharaohs were buried with beautiful, expensive treasure, many people have disturbed their graves to rob them of their wealth.

A GOLD MASK FROM TUTANKHAMUN'S TOMB

Lord Carnarvon (right) and Howard Carter (kneeling) pictured opening pharaoh Tutankhamun's tomb. Carter later died suddenly from a mosquito bite on his neck. Spookily, a similar wound was later found on the body of Tutankhamun!

THE VALLEY OF THE KINGS

Mysteriously, at the exact time of Lord Carnarvon's death, all the lights went out in Cairo. Also, on the day the tomb was opened, a cobra ate Carter's pet canary. The cobra is a symbol of the goddess Wadjet, protector of the kings and queens of Egypt. Was that the pharaoh seeking revenge?

People have reported seeing a pharaoh in a chariot charging through the valley at midnight! He is said to wear a gold collar and headdress, and is pulled by several ghostly black horses. Visitors have also reported hearing ghostly footsteps, screams, and shuffling.

Greyfriars Churchyard, Scotland

December 1998, Edinburgh, Scotland. A homeless man was looking for shelter from the pouring rain. He wandered into Greyfriars Churchyard and broke into an old mausoleum. Down the dark, stone staircase he found four wooden coffins. The man smashed them open hoping to find some valuables. Suddenly, a hole opened beneath him and he fell into a pit below. The pit had been used to bury **plague** victims hundreds of years ago. Their terrifying corpses covered in stinking slime sent the man screaming from the tomb!

Since that night in 1998, Greyfriars Churchyard has become one of the most haunted places in the world!

The mausoleum held the body of Sir George MacKenzie. MacKenzie had organized the torture and deaths of a Scottish religious group known as the **Covenanters.** He also imprisoned hundreds of Covenanters in an open-air prison at Greyfriars. Most of the prisoners died from starvation, disease, or cold!

Have some evil spirits now been let loose? Since 1998, some people near the mausoleum have felt invisible hands try to strangle them. Others have had their hair pulled, or felt as if they have been punched or kicked! Unexplained bruises, scratches, and burns have appeared on people's skin. Fires have started nearby for no reason. A large number of dead wildlife has been found near the mausoleum, too.

The Jewish Cemetery, Czech Republic

Jewish people in Prague weren't allowed to bury their dead outside the Jewish Quarter. Their faith also forbade moving headstones. When their small cemetery was full, the people had a problem. They solved this by putting a layer of dirt on top of the old graves and burying people on top. There are now around 100,000 bodies buried in 12 layers of graves! As some believe building on a cemetery creates restless spirits, there must be a few ghosts at this cemetery.

MANY OF THE OLD HEADSTONES COMMEMORATE SOMEONE BURIED SEVERAL LAYERS FURTHER DOWN.

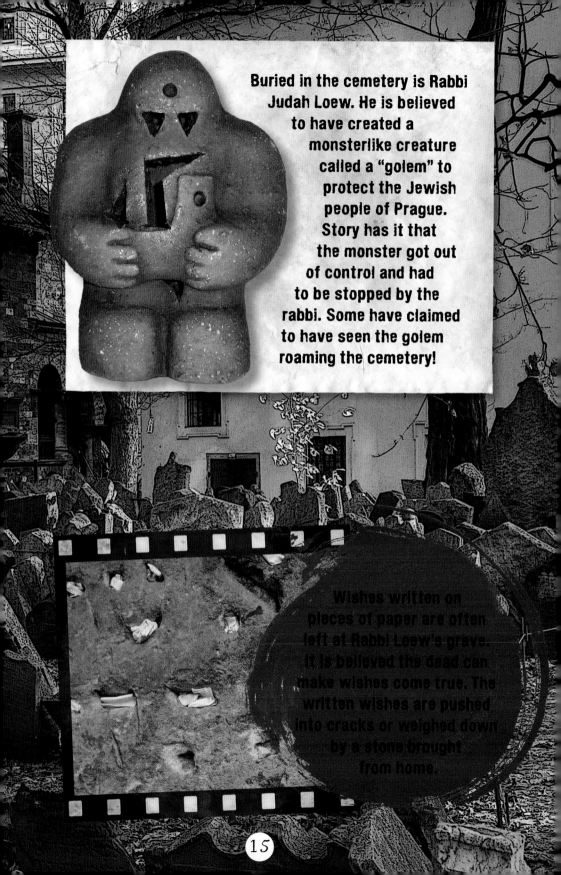

Buried in the cemetery is Rabbi Judah Loew. He is believed to have created a monsterlike creature called a "golem" to protect the Jewish people of Prague. Story has it that the monster got out of control and had to be stopped by the rabbi. Some have claimed to have seen the golem roaming the cemetery!

Wishes written on pieces of paper are often left at Rabbi Loew's grave. It is believed the dead can make wishes come true. The written wishes are pushed into cracks or weighed down by a stone brought from home.

Capuchin Catacombs, Italy

One of the most nightmarish cemeteries in the world has to be the Capuchin Catacombs in Sicily. In 1599, the Capuchin monks **mummified** brother Silvestro and placed him in the catacombs. His 400-year-old mummy still greets people at the entrance! Since then, around 8,000 mummies have been created to line the walls of the catacombs.

Wealthy people would pay for a niche in the catacombs to be displayed in. When their family stopped paying, their remains would often be put on a shelf!

THE MONKS' CORRIDOR

Most of the bodies, dressed in their Sunday best, are hung along the walls on hooks! Some are placed in caskets. One little girl kept in a display case died in 1920. She was the last person buried here and is so well-preserved she looks as if she is sleeping. Most of the mummies are starting to **decay**. They look terrifying as they stare down at visitors.

The mummies are placed in different areas depending on who they were. There are sections for monks, professors, men, women, and children.

The Merry Graveyard, Romania

You wouldn't think a graveyard could be a happy place. At the Merry Graveyard the graves are not marked with cold, gray stone, but with brightly painted, carved wooden crosses! Each cross is decorated with a painting and a poem that tell something about the person buried beneath it. Some of the verses are funny, but others are heartbreaking. A local carpenter started painting the crosses around 1935. Now one of his assistants has taken over the task.

Although the cemetery looks bright and cheerful, it is a little unsettling to look at the colorful portraits and read the often sad verses about the people buried there. On the grave of Pop Grigore, the verse goes:

All my life I was miserable and sad
Because my father left me when
    I was just a child
Maybe this was my fate
To die young

One poem tells of
a 3-year-old girl killed
in a car accident:
"Of all the places in this country
You had to stop right here.
By my house you hit me so
And sent me to the death below
And left my parents full of woe."

Highgate Cemetery, England

Opened in 1839, Highgate Cemetery became the most popular burial spot in London. Around 170,000 people are buried there. By the 1960s the cemetery had been abandoned. The graves became overgrown and the cemetery fell into disrepair. It is a very creepy place. Decaying statues of the dead, angels, and animals peer out from the undergrowth.

There have been many reported ghost sightings. A man whose car broke down near the cemetery saw glowing red eyes staring at him through the cemetery gates. The ghost of an old woman has been seen running through the graveyard searching for her children that she is said to have murdered. A dark figure has been seen standing, staring into space. When approached, the figure vanishes and reappears a short distance away.

One of the graveyard's most famous ghosts is the "Highgate **Vampire**." The tall ghostly figure in a top hat has been seen walking in the cemetery. People believed that a vampire from Romania had been brought to Highgate in a coffin in the early 1700s. The ghost was believed to be a vampire looking for victims!

La Noria Cemetery, Chile

Humberstone, Chile, was once a thriving mining town. It had a gruesome history of forced labor and slavery. Many died while working at the mines. The dead were buried at the nearby cemetery of La Noria. Local villagers now believe that Humberstone is haunted by the dead. Many people believe that when the sun sets, the dead rise up from the cemetery and walk around the town. Some people have claimed to have seen such ghosts.

Human bones have been found scattered around the abandoned town. Some believe this is proof that the corpses rise up out of their graves.

THE ABANDONED MINING TOWN OF HUMBERSTONE

La Noria cemetery (right) has been named one of the most frightening places in the world. Graves have been opened and bodies dressed in their burial clothes are sometimes found lying around the cemetery.

The deserted town's schoolroom (below) is the site of several ghost sightings. Children have been heard playing or screaming. People have even reported seeing ghost children sitting at their school desks!

THE SCHOOLROOM

The Hanging Coffins, The Philippines

The Igorot people of the Philippines do not bury their elders. Instead, they place them in hanging coffins high up on a rock face! It is believed this brings them closer to heaven. It protects the corpse from headhunters, animals, and the damp soil, too. The custom also leaves the land free for growing crops.

The Igorot buried their bodies curled up like newborn babies. They would break the corpses' bones to get them to fit into the small coffins!

HANGING COFFINS AT SAGADA

Sometimes a chair is hung with the coffin. The body of a dead elder was placed on a special "death chair." Relatives would come and pay their last respects. After several days, the body is put in its coffin. Workers hammer in supports on the cliff face to rest the coffin on. People fight to lift the coffin in place. It is thought to be good luck to get covered in the dead person's blood!

The elders would usually carve their own coffins before they died. Sometimes, decaying coffins fall from the rocks, scattering their horrifying contents over the valley. The area is said to be haunted. Local residents have heard whispering voices, groans, and have seen strange shadows in the area.

Howard Street Cemetery, Salem

Salem is famous for its history of witch-hunting. From 1692 to 1693 over 200 people were accused of **witchcraft**! Two girls age 9 and 11 began to have twitching fits and accused three people in the village of practicing witchcraft. Soon hundreds of people were being accused. Salem started to have witch trials, to try to prove who was and was not a witch.

THE CEMETERY WITH THE JAIL IN THE BACKGROUND

The trials were not at all fair. Several innocent people were put to death. Some more falsely suspected witches died in jail. When a popular elderly man, Giles Corey, was accused of witchcraft, he refused to say he was guilty or not guilty. He was "pressed" to force him to plead. Heavy stones were placed on him to force a confession. He died after two days and is said to have cursed the village with his dying breath. He is believed to be buried where he was pressed, in the Howard Street Cemetery. He is now said to haunt the cemetery and the town.

The ghost of Giles Corey is said to appear in Salem each time a disaster is about to strike the town. He was spotted on the night of June 24th, 1914. The following day a huge fire destroyed most of Salem!

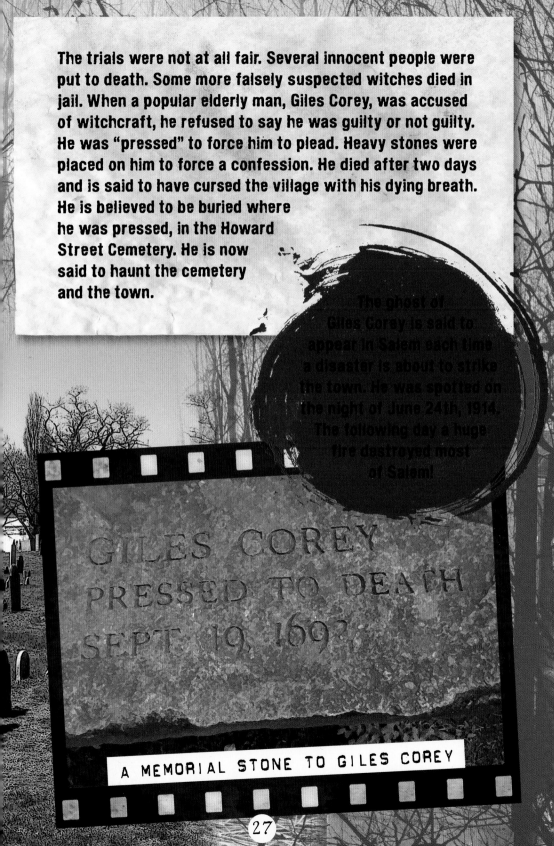

A MEMORIAL STONE TO GILES COREY

Daksa Island, Croatia

Often called "the island of ghosts," Daksa Island lies just 1.6 miles (2.7 km) off the coast of the beautiful city of Dubrovnik, Croatia. Once home to a monastery, it is now completely deserted. The many island-hopping tourist boat trips that leave Dubrovnik deliberately avoid the island. Why? The island was the scene of a brutal massacre in 1944.

Near the end of World War II, anti-Nazi forces in the region began to round up people they suspected of helping the Germans. They rowed them out to the deserted Daksa Island.

DAKSA ISLAND

DESERTED BUILDINGS AT DAKSA ISLAND

The suspects were shot by firing squad, on the island. It is believed they were not given any trial. The mayor of Dubrovnik and even the local priest were among those shot.

After the massacre, stories soon spread that the island was haunted. These stories may have been invented to keep people from finding the bodies, which were never buried. Finally, in 2009, the remains of 53 men were found in two locations on the island. In June 2010 the bodies were re-buried on Daksa. Some believe this proper burial may now stop them from haunting the island.

Glossary

casket A coffin.

Covenanters A Scottish religious group that was against religious interference by ruling Kings.

decay To gradually fall apart.

haunted To be visited by a ghost.

lure To tempt or lead away.

mausoleums Large, fancy tombs.

mummified Embalmed so as to become a mummy.

Nazi Members of a German fascist party controlling Germany from 1933 to 1945.

orb Something in the shape of a ball.

pharaohs The rulers of ancient Egypt.

plague A serious disease causing a high rate of death.

vampire The body of a dead person believed to come from the grave at night and suck the blood of sleeping persons.

vandals A person who destroys or damages property on purpose.

witchcraft The use of sorcery or magic.

Further Information

Chandler, Matt. *Bachelor's Grove Cemetery and Other Haunted Places of the Midwest (Haunted America)*. North Mankato, MN: Capstone Press, 2014.

Summers, Alex. *Haunted Battlefields and Cemeteries (Yikes! It's Haunted)*. Vero Beach, FL: Rourke Publishing Group, 2016.

Website

Kidzworld information about the Salem Witch Trials: **www.kidzworld.com/article/2536-the-salem-witch -trials-of-1692**

Publisher's note to educators and parents:
Our editors have carefully reviewed these websites to ensure that they are suitable for students. Many websites change frequently, however, and we cannot guarantee that a site's future contents will continue to meet our high standards of quality and educational value. Be advised that students should be closely supervised whenever they access the Internet.

Index

Don't be scared! Most people don't believe ghosts are real at all. No one has ever scientifically proven they exist. But it can be fun to get yourself a little spooked!